Items should be returned on or before the last date
shown below. Items not already requested by other
borrowers may be renewed in person, in writing or by
telephone. To renew, please quote the number on the
barcode label. To renew online a PIN is required.
This can be requested at your local library.
Renew online @ **www.dublincitypubliclibraries.ie**
Fines charged for overdue items will include postage
incurred in recovery. Damage to or loss of items will
be charged to the borrower.

**Leabharlanna Poiblí Chathair Bhaile Átha Cliath**
**Dublin City Public Libraries**

Marino Branch
Brainse Marglann Mhuiríne
Tel: 8336297

**Dublin City**
Baile Átha Cliath

| Date Due | Date Due | Date Due |
|----------|----------|----------|
|          | 23 /9/2011 |        |
|          |          |          |

# 1 mix, 50 cakes

## Christine France

LOVE FOOD

First published in 2009
Love Food ® is an imprint of Parragon Books Ltd

Parragon
Queen Street House
4 Queen Street
Bath BA1 1HE, UK

ISBN: 978-1-4075-6437-1

Printed in China

Written by Christine France
Internal design by Simon Levy
Photography by Clive Streeter
Home economy by Angela Drake

Notes for the Reader
This book uses both metric and imperial measurements. Follow
the same units of measurement throughout; do not mix metric and
imperial. All spoon measurements are level: teaspoons are assumed
to be 5 ml, and tablespoons are assumed to be 15 ml. Unless
otherwise stated, milk is assumed to be full fat, eggs and individual
vegetables are medium, and pepper is freshly ground black pepper.

The times given are an approximate guide only. Preparation times
differ according to the techniques used by different people and the
cooking times may also vary from those given. Optional ingredients,
variations or serving suggestions have not been included in the
calculations.

Recipes using raw or very lightly cooked eggs should be avoided
by infants, the elderly, pregnant women, convalescents and anyone
suffering from an illness. Pregnant and breastfeeding women are
advised to avoid eating peanuts and peanut products. Sufferers
from nut allergies should be aware that some of the ready-made
ingredients used in the recipes in this book may contain nuts.
Always check the packaging before use.

# Contents

# Introduction

Even if you're not a domestic god or goddess, the good news is that home-baked cakes don't have to be difficult or time-consuming. This book is packed with quick-mix cakes for all occasions, so you'll never be short of ideas for easy, irresistible home-baked treats. The beauty of this book is that every single recipe is based on the Basic Cake Mix (see page 8). To make life easier for you, we have done the hard work so that each recipe is complete and you won't need to refer back to the basic recipe every time.

## Equipment

The equipment needed for these cakes is found in most kitchens: mixing bowl, sieve, weighing scales, measuring spoons and jug, a wire rack and cake tins.

Good-quality cake tins conduct heat evenly and efficiently for perfect results and will last for years. Basic cake tin shapes include deep round and square, sandwich, ring, Bundt, loaf, spring release and rectangular, and bun or muffin trays. Since cake tin sizes vary between manufacturers, many of the recipes in this book provide the tin's capacity. To find a tin's capacity, simply use a measuring jug to pour water into the tin and note how much liquid it takes to fill the tin.

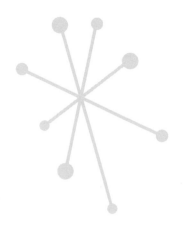

Mixing bowls in tempered glass or plastic are tough and versatile for mixing. Choose measuring jugs and spoons marked clearly in standard measures.

A hand-held electric mixer does much of the hard work but you can mix by hand with a wooden spoon if you prefer.

## Basic Ingredients

The basic cake mix includes plain flour, baking powder, butter/oil/cream/yogurt, sugar/honey/syrup, eggs, vanilla or other flavouring extract, and milk or fruit juice.

Plain flour is used with baking powder, and these must be sifted together to ensure even distribution of the raising agent throughout the mixture. Ratios do vary slightly so always check the quantities in the ingredients list before you start.

Butter gives the best flavour, but it can be replaced by margarine if you prefer. Spreads are usually lower in fat and may give unreliable results. Use softened butter, either at room temperature and beaten until soft, or softened in a microwave for a few seconds but not melted. Oil is useful when a moist texture is required, such as for gingerbreads, and light-flavoured oil, such as sunflower, is a good choice. Cream and yogurt are lower in fat than butter, so these produce cakes with a denser texture and a shorter life.

Either white or golden caster sugar give a light, fine textured cake, but natural light or dark muscovado sugar can also be substituted to add an extra richness of flavour. Always ensure there are no hard lumps in the sugar before adding to the mix as these may not dissolve. Golden syrup or honey can be used as a substitute for sugar in cakes where a softer texture is required. Demerara sugar is good for sprinkling over the top to add a crunchy topping. Icing sugar is invaluable for fillings and icings, or for dusting over cakes as instant decoration.

Eggs should be medium, ideally at room temperature. If you store eggs in the refrigerator, remove them about 30 minutes before use to allow them to come up to room temperature.

Vanilla extract is the most versatile flavouring to enhance cakes and bakes. For true flavour, make sure to choose bottles marked 'extract' rather than 'flavouring'. Other useful extracts used in this book are almond, coffee, orange flower water, rose water and peppermint.

Milk or fruit juice is added to lighten the mix, and you can choose whole, semi-skimmed or skimmed milk, or fruit juices like apple, orange or lemon. Some recipes may omit this, depending on the balance of added ingredients.

## Extra Ingredients

Wholemeal flour, oats or polenta may be substituted for some or all of the white flour or added to the mix to vary the texture and flavour, the amount depending on the balance of other ingredients. Generally, the higher the fibre and coarser the grain, the denser the resulting texture will be.

The simplest way to vary the flavour of cakes is to add spices – cinnamon, mixed spice, allspice, nutmeg, ginger or star anise all work well in cakes. Sift the spices with the flour and baking powder to ensure they're evenly combined with the mix. Finely grated citrus rind will add a light, fresh flavour to many cakes and frostings.

Chocolate cakes are always a favourite and this may be added in the form of cocoa powder, chocolate chips or melted chocolate. It may be necessary to reduce the flour quantity when adding cocoa to some cakes, so make sure to check the recipe.

Fresh or dried fruits transform a simple sponge into a rich special-occasion cake or luxurious gateau. Dried fruits have a concentrated flavour and sweetness and they're great storecupboard standbys. Canned fruit should be drained well, as the extra liquid may upset the balance of ingredients.

Nuts (such as almonds, hazelnuts, walnuts or pecans) or seeds (such as sunflower, pumpkin, poppy or sesame) not only give a crunchy texture to cakes but also add valuable nutrients and fibre for healthier treats.

## Top Tips for Successful Cakes

- Turn on the oven before you start in order to preheat it to the correct temperature whilst you're mixing.

- Brush cake tins with melted butter or oil and line with non-stick baking paper to prevent sticking.

- Measure ingredients accurately and level measuring spoons flat with the back of a knife.

- Avoid over-mixing because this can cause a heavy texture – beat the mix until just smooth

- Bake the cake immediately once mixed because the baking powder begins to act as soon as it's combined with liquid.

- Avoid opening the oven door too often during baking – this reduces the oven temperature and can cause cakes to sink.

- Test cakes carefully for doneness – they should be well risen and golden brown and starting to shrink from the sides of the tin. Sponge cakes should feel springy to the touch.

- To prevent damage, allow cakes to stand in the tin to firm up for a few minutes before turning out onto a wire rack to finish cooling.

# Basic Cake Mix

**Makes 2 x 20-cm/8-inch sponge sandwich cakes**

* oil or melted butter, for greasing
* 175 g/6 oz plain white flour
* 1 tbsp baking powder
* 175 g/6 oz unsalted butter, softened (recipes may substitute oil, cream or yogurt)
* 175 g/6 oz caster sugar (recipes may substitute golden caster, light or dark muscovado sugars, or honey/syrup)
* 3 eggs
* 1 tsp vanilla extract (recipes may substitute other flavouring extracts, e.g. almond, coffee, orange flower water)
* 2 tbsp milk or fruit juice

This is the basic recipe that all 50 variations of cakes in the book are based on.

For each recipe the basic mix is highlighted ( * ) for easy reference, so all you have to do is follow the easy steps each time and you'll never run out of ideas for creative cakes.

Please note that the basic ingredients may vary from time to time so please check these carefully.

# Favourites

# Chocolate Sandwich Cake

1. Preheat the oven to 180°C/350°F/Gas Mark 4. Grease two 20-cm/8-inch sandwich cake tins and line the bases with baking paper.

2. Sift the flour, cocoa and baking powder into a large bowl and add the butter, caster sugar, eggs and vanilla extract. Beat well until the mixture is smooth, then stir in the milk.

3. Divide the mixture between the prepared tins and smooth the surfaces with a palette knife. Bake in the preheated oven for 25–30 minutes, or until well risen and firm to the touch. Leave to cool in the tins for 2–3 minutes, then turn out and finish cooling on a wire rack.

4. When the cakes have cooled completely, sandwich together with the chocolate spread, then dust with icing sugar and serve.

**Serves 8**

* oil or melted butter, for greasing
  150 g/5½ oz plain white flour
  2 tbsp cocoa powder
* 1 tbsp baking powder
* 175 g/6 oz unsalted butter, softened
* 175 g/6 oz golden caster sugar
* 3 eggs, beaten
* 1 tsp vanilla extract
* 2 tbsp milk
  140 g/5 oz chocolate spread
  icing sugar, for dusting

# Coffee & Walnut Ring

1. Preheat the oven to 160°C/325°F/Gas Mark 3. Grease a 1.5-litre/2¾-pint ring cake tin, preferably non-stick.

2. Sift the flour and baking powder into a large bowl and add the butter, sugar, eggs and coffee extract. Beat well until the mixture is smooth, then stir in the chopped walnuts.

3. Spoon the mixture into the prepared tin and smooth the surface with a palette knife. Bake in the preheated oven for 40–45 minutes, or until risen, firm and golden brown.

4. Leave to cool in the tin for 10 minutes, then turn out carefully onto a wire rack. Whilst the cake is still warm, spoon over half the maple syrup. Leave to cool completely. To serve, top with walnut halves and drizzle over the remaining maple syrup.

**Serves 10**

* oil or melted butter, for greasing
* 175 g/6 oz plain white flour
* 1 tbsp baking powder
* 175 g/6 oz unsalted butter, softened
* 175 g/6 oz light muscovado sugar
* 3 eggs, beaten
* 1 tsp coffee extract
* 70 g/2½ oz walnuts, chopped, plus extra walnut halves to decorate
* 4 tbsp maple syrup

# Sticky Ginger Loaf

1. Preheat the oven to 180°C/350°F/Gas Mark 4. Grease and line a 1.2-litre/2-pint loaf tin.

2. Sift the flour, baking powder and ground ginger into a large bowl. Add the oil, sugar, golden syrup and eggs, then beat well to a smooth batter. Stir in the chopped ginger.

3. Pour the mixture into the prepared tin. Bake in the preheated oven for 1–1¼ hours, until well risen and firm.

4. Leave to cool in the tin for 10 minutes, then turn out and finish cooling on a wire rack. To serve, brush the top of the cake with the ginger syrup, decorate with sliced ginger and cut into slices.

**Serves 8–10**

- oil or melted butter, for greasing
- 175 g/6 oz plain white flour
- 1 tbsp baking powder
- 1 tbsp ground ginger
- 175 ml/6 fl oz sunflower oil
- 85 g/3 oz dark muscovado sugar
- 85 g/3 oz golden syrup
- 3 eggs, beaten
- 3 pieces stem ginger in syrup, drained and finely chopped, plus 2 tbsp syrup from the jar
- sliced stem ginger, to decorate

# Marbled Chocolate & Vanilla Ring

1. Preheat the oven to 160°C/325°F/Gas Mark 3. Grease a 1.5-litre/2¾-pint ring cake tin, preferably non-stick.

2. Sift the flour and baking powder into a large bowl and add the butter, caster sugar and eggs. Beat well until the mixture is smooth. Transfer half the mixture to a separate bowl.

3. Mix the cocoa powder with the milk and stir into one bowl of mixture. Add the vanilla extract to the other bowl and mix evenly. Spoon alternate tablespoons of the two mixtures into the prepared tin and swirl lightly with a palette knife for a marbled effect.

4. Bake in the preheated oven for 40–50 minutes, or until risen, firm and golden brown. Leave to cool in the tin for 10 minutes, then turn out and finish cooling on a wire rack. Dust with icing sugar before serving.

**Serves 12**

* oil or melted butter, for greasing
* 175 g/6 oz plain white flour
* 1 tbsp baking powder
* 175 g/6 oz unsalted butter, softened
* 175 g/6 oz caster sugar
* 3 eggs, beaten
  2 tbsp cocoa powder
* 2 tbsp milk
* 1 tsp vanilla extract
  icing sugar, for dusting

# Sponge Roll

1. Preheat the oven to 180°C/350°F/Gas Mark 4. Grease and line a 23 x 33-cm/9 x 13-inch Swiss roll tin with the paper 1 cm/½ inch above the rim. Lay a sheet of baking paper on the work surface and sprinkle with caster sugar.

2. Sift the flour and baking powder into a large bowl and add the butter, sugar, eggs and vanilla extract. Beat well until the mixture is smooth, then beat in the milk.

3. Spoon the mixture into the prepared tin and smooth into the corners with a palette knife. Bake in the preheated oven for 15–20 minutes, or until risen, firm and golden brown.

4. When cooked, turn the sponge out onto the sugared baking paper and spread with jam. Roll up the sponge firmly from one short side to enclose the jam, keeping the paper around the outside to hold it in place.

5. Lift onto a wire rack to cool, removing the paper when firm. Sprinkle with caster sugar, cut into slices and serve.

**Serves 8**

* oil or melted butter, for greasing
150 g/5½ oz plain white flour
1½ tsp baking powder
* 175 g/6 oz unsalted butter, softened
* 175 g/6 oz caster sugar, plus extra for sprinkling
* 3 eggs, beaten
* 1 tsp vanilla extract
* 2 tbsp milk
115 g/4 oz raspberry jam, warmed

# Date & Spice Loaf

1. Preheat the oven to 160°C/325°F/Gas Mark 3. Grease and line a 1.3-litre/2¼-pint loaf tin.

2. Sift the flours, baking powder and mixed spice into a large bowl, adding any bran left in the sieve. Add the butter, sugar, eggs and vanilla extract. Beat well until the mixture is smooth, then stir in half the dates.

3. Spoon the mixture into the prepared tin and scatter over the remaining dates. Bake in the preheated oven for 40–50 minutes, or until risen and golden brown.

4. Leave to cool in the tin for 10 minutes, then turn out and finish cooling on a wire rack.

**Serves 8–10**

* oil or melted butter, for greasing
85 g/3 oz plain white flour
100 g/3½ oz plain wholemeal flour
* 1 tbsp baking powder
1 tsp ground mixed spice
* 175 g/6 oz unsalted butter, softened
* 175 g/6 oz golden caster sugar
* 3 eggs, beaten
* 1 tsp vanilla extract
175 g/6 oz stoned dates, roughly chopped

# Country Fruit Cake

1. Preheat the oven to 160°C/325°F/Gas Mark 3. Grease and line a 20-cm/8-inch round deep cake tin.

2. Sift the flours, baking powder and nutmeg into a large bowl, adding any bran left in the sieve. Add the butter, muscovado sugar, eggs and vanilla extract. Beat well until the mixture is smooth, then stir in the milk and mixed dried fruit.

3. Spoon the mixture into the prepared tin and smooth level with a palette knife. Sprinkle the demerara sugar evenly over the surface. Bake in the preheated oven for 1 hour 20 minutes–1 hour 30 minutes, or until risen, firm and golden brown.

4. Leave to cool in the tin for about 20 minutes, then turn out and finish cooling on a wire rack.

**Serves 10**

* oil or melted butter, for greasing
* 175 g/6 oz plain white flour
  70 g/2½ oz plain wholemeal flour
  2 tsp baking powder
  ½ tsp ground nutmeg
* 175 g/6 oz unsalted butter, softened
* 175 g/6 oz light muscovado sugar
* 3 eggs, beaten
* 1 tsp vanilla extract
  1 tbsp milk
  200 g/7 oz mixed dried fruit
  1 tbsp demerara sugar

# Vanilla Victoria Sponge Cake

1. Preheat the oven to 180°C/350°F/Gas Mark 4. Grease two 20-cm/8-inch sandwich cake tins and line the bases with baking paper.

2. Sift the flour and baking powder into a large bowl and add the butter, caster sugar, eggs and vanilla extract. Beat well until the mixture is smooth, then stir in the milk.

3. Divide the mixture between the prepared tins and smooth the surfaces with a palette knife. Bake in the preheated oven for 25–30 minutes, or until risen, firm and golden brown. Leave to cool in the tins for 2–3 minutes, then turn out and finish cooling on a wire rack.

4. For the buttercream filling, beat together the butter, icing sugar and vanilla extract until smooth. Spread the bottom of one cake with the strawberry jam and spread the top of the other cake with the buttercream, then sandwich the two together to enclose the filling, pressing down lightly.

5. Sprinkle with icing sugar before serving.

**Serves 6–8**

* oil or melted butter, for greasing
* 175 g/6 oz plain white flour
* 1 tbsp baking powder
* 175 g/6 oz unsalted butter, softened
* 175 g/6 oz golden caster sugar
* 3 eggs, beaten
* 1 tsp vanilla extract
* 2 tbsp milk

**Filling**
55 g/2 oz unsalted butter, softened
115 g/4 oz icing sugar, plus extra for dusting
½ tsp vanilla extract
3 tbsp strawberry jam

# Carrot Cake with Orange Frosting

1. Preheat the oven to 160°C/325°F/Gas Mark 3. Grease and line a 23-cm/9-inch round deep cake tin.

2. Sift the flour, baking powder, cinnamon and ginger into a bowl and add the butter, muscovado sugar and eggs. Beat well until smooth, then stir in the orange juice, carrots and chopped pecan nuts.

3. Spoon the mixture into the prepared tin and spread the top level. Bake in the preheated oven for 1 hour–1 hour 10 minutes, or until well risen, firm and golden brown.

4. Leave to cool in the tin for 10 minutes, then turn out onto a wire rack to finish cooling.

5. For the frosting, place all the ingredients in a bowl and beat until smooth and thick, adding more orange juice if necessary. Spread over the top of the cake and decorate with pecan halves.

**Serves 10**

- oil or melted butter, for greasing
- 175 g/6 oz plain white flour
- 1 tbsp baking powder
- 1 tsp ground cinnamon
- ½ tsp ground ginger
- 175 g/6 oz unsalted butter, softened
- 175 g/6 oz light muscovado sugar
- 3 eggs, beaten
- 2 tbsp orange juice
- 200 g/7 oz carrots, coarsely grated
- 55 g/2 oz pecan nuts, chopped, plus extra pecan halves to decorate

**Frosting**

55 g/2 oz full-fat soft cheese

250 g/9 oz icing sugar

finely grated rind of 1 orange

1 tbsp orange juice, plus extra if needed

# Lemon Drizzle Loaf

1. Preheat the oven to 180°C/350°F/Gas Mark 4. Grease and line a 1.2-litre/2-pint loaf tin.

2. Sift the flour and baking powder into a large bowl and add the butter, caster sugar, eggs and egg yolk. Beat well until the mixture is smooth, then stir in the lemon rind and juice.

3. Spoon the mixture into the prepared tin and smooth the surface with a palette knife. Bake in the preheated oven for 40–50 minutes, or until well risen and golden brown.

4. Remove the tin from the oven and transfer to a wire rack. For the syrup, place the icing sugar and lemon juice in a saucepan and heat gently without boiling, stirring until the sugar dissolves.

5. Prick the top of the loaf several times with a skewer and spoon over the syrup. Leave to cool completely in the tin, then turn out, scatter with strips of lemon zest and cut into slices.

**Serves 8–10**

* oil or melted butter,
   for greasing
* 175 g/6 oz plain white flour
* 1 tbsp baking powder
* 175 g/6 oz unsalted butter,
   softened
* 175 g/6 oz golden caster sugar
* 3 eggs, beaten
  1 egg yolk
  finely grated rind of 1 lemon
* 2 tbsp lemon juice
  fine strips of lemon zest,
   to decorate

**Syrup**
85 g/3 oz icing sugar
3 tbsp lemon juice

# Special

# Birthday Number Cake

1. Preheat the oven to 160°C/325°F/Gas Mark 3. Grease and line a 25 x 18-cm/10 x 7-inch numeral cake tin or a frame on a baking sheet, about 5 cm/2 inches deep.

2. Sift the flour and baking powder into a large bowl and add the butter, caster sugar, eggs and vanilla extract. Beat well until the mixture is smooth, then stir in the orange juice and rind.

3. Spoon the mixture into the prepared tin and smooth the surface with a palette knife. Bake in the preheated oven for 40–50 minutes, or until risen, firm and golden brown. Leave to cool in the tin for 5 minutes, then turn out and finish cooling on a wire rack.

4. For the frosting, beat together the icing sugar, butter, orange rind and juice until smooth. Spread over the cake evenly, smoothing with a palette knife.

5. Arrange the orange slices on top of the cake to decorate, then add the birthday candles and serve.

**Serves 10–12**

* oil or melted butter, for greasing
* 175 g/6 oz plain white flour
* 1 tbsp baking powder
* 175 g/6 oz unsalted butter, softened
* 175 g/6 oz caster sugar
* 3 eggs, beaten
* 1 tsp vanilla extract
* 2 tbsp orange juice
  finely grated rind of ½ orange
  sugar orange slices and birthday candles, to decorate

**Frosting**
350 g/12 oz icing sugar, sifted
175 g/6 oz unsalted butter, softened
finely grated rind of ½ orange
1 tbsp orange juice

# White Chocolate Valentine's Gateau

1. Preheat the oven to 160°C/325°F/Gas Mark 3. Grease a 1.5-litre/2¾-pint heart-shaped cake tin.

2. Sift the flour and baking powder into a bowl and add the butter, sugar, eggs and vanilla extract. Beat well until smooth, then stir in the grated chocolate.

3. Spoon the mixture into the prepared tin and smooth the surface with a palette knife. Bake in the preheated oven for 45–55 minutes, or until risen, firm and golden brown. Leave to cool in the tin for 10 minutes, then turn out onto a wire rack to finish cooling.

4. For the frosting, melt the chocolate with the milk in a heatproof bowl set over a pan of hot water. Remove from the heat and stir until smooth, then leave to cool for 10 minutes. Whip the cream until it holds soft peaks, then fold into the cooled chocolate mixture.

5. Sprinkle the cake with the rum, if using. Spread the frosting over the top and sides of the cake, swirling with a palette knife, then decorate with crystallised violets.

**Serves 10**

* oil or melted butter, for greasing
* 175 g/6 oz plain white flour
* 1 tbsp baking powder
* 175 g/6 oz unsalted butter, softened
* 175 g/6 oz caster sugar
* 3 eggs, beaten
* 1 tsp vanilla extract
  55 g/2 oz white chocolate, grated
  2 tbsp white rum (optional)
  crystallised violets, to decorate

**Frosting**
200 g/7 oz white chocolate, broken into pieces
2 tbsp milk
200 ml/7 fl oz double cream

# Rich Chocolate Rum Torte

1. Preheat the oven to 180°C/350°F/Gas Mark 4. Grease and line three 18-cm/7-inch sandwich cake tins.

2. Place the chocolate and milk in a small saucepan and heat gently, without boiling, until melted. Stir and remove from the heat.

3. Sift the flour and baking powder into a large bowl and add the butter, sugar, eggs and vanilla extract. Beat well until smooth, then stir in the chocolate mixture.

4. Divide the mixture between the prepared tins and smooth the tops level. Bake in the preheated oven for 20–25 minutes, until risen and firm to the touch.

5. Leave to cool in the tins for 5 minutes, then turn out and finish cooling on wire racks.

6. For the frosting, melt the chocolate with the cream and rum in a small saucepan over a low heat. Remove from the heat and leave to cool, stirring occasionally, until it reaches a spreadable consistency.

7. Sandwich the cakes together with about a third of the frosting, then spread the remainder over the top and sides of the cake, swirling with a palette knife. Sprinkle with chocolate curls or grated chocolate and leave to set.

## Serves 8

- oil or melted butter, for greasing
- 70 g/2½ oz plain chocolate, broken into pieces
- 2 tbsp milk
- 175 g/6 oz plain white flour
- 1 tbsp baking powder
- 175 g/6 oz unsalted butter, softened
- 175 g/6 oz dark muscovado sugar
- 3 eggs, beaten
- 1 tsp vanilla extract
- chocolate curls or grated chocolate, to decorate

### Frosting
- 225 g/8 oz plain chocolate, broken into pieces
- 225 ml/8 fl oz double cream
- 2 tbsp dark rum

# Frosted Raspberry Almond Ring

1. Preheat the oven to 160°C/325°F/Gas Mark 3. Grease a 1.5-litre/2¾-pint ring cake tin, preferably non-stick.

2. Sift the flour and baking powder into a large bowl and add the butter, caster sugar, eggs and almond extract. Beat well until the mixture is smooth, then stir in the ground almonds. Mash half the raspberries with a fork and stir into the mixture.

3. Spoon the mixture into the prepared tin and smooth the surface with a palette knife. Bake in the preheated oven for 40–45 minutes or until risen, firm and golden brown.

4. Leave to cool in the tin for 10 minutes, then turn out carefully onto a wire rack to finish cooling.

5. For the frosting, place the egg white, icing sugar, golden syrup and cream of tartar in a bowl over a saucepan of hot water and whisk vigorously with a hand-held electric mixer until thick enough to hold its shape.

6. Swirl the frosting over the top of the cake. Decorate with the remaining raspberries and the flaked almonds.

## Serves 8–10

* oil or melted butter, for greasing
* 175 g/6 oz plain white flour
* 1 tbsp baking powder
* 175 g/6 oz unsalted butter, softened
* 175 g/6 oz caster sugar
* 3 eggs, beaten
* 1 tsp almond extract
* 70 g/2½ oz ground almonds
* 225 g/8 oz fresh raspberries
* toasted flaked almonds, to decorate

### Frosting
1 large egg white
140 g/5 oz icing sugar
1 tbsp golden syrup
¼ tsp cream of tartar

# Glazed Fruit & Nut Cake

1. Preheat the oven to 160°C/325°F/Gas Mark 3. Grease a 23-cm/9-inch round spring-release cake tin and sprinkle with a little flour to coat, shaking out the excess.

2. Sift the flour, baking powder and mixed spice into a large bowl and add the butter, sugar, eggs and vanilla extract. Beat well until the mixture is smooth, then stir in the milk, mixed dried fruit and chopped mixed nuts.

3. Spoon the mixture into the tin and smooth the surface with a palette knife. Bake in the preheated oven for about 1 hour, or until risen, firm and golden brown.

4. Leave to cool in the tin for 30 minutes, then remove the sides and place on a wire rack to finish cooling.

5. Brush the top of the cake with a little of the warmed honey then arrange the glacé fruits and whole shelled nuts on top. Brush with the remaining honey and leave to set.

**Serves 16–18**

* oil or melted butter, for greasing
* 250 g/9 oz plain white flour, plus extra for sprinkling
* 1 tbsp baking powder
* 1 tsp ground mixed spice
* 175 g/6 oz unsalted butter, softened
* 175 g/6 oz dark muscovado sugar
* 3 eggs, beaten
* 1 tsp vanilla extract
* 2 tbsp milk
* 300 g/10½ oz mixed dried fruit
* 85 g/3 oz chopped mixed nuts

To decorate
* 3 tbsp clear honey, warmed
* 350 g/12 oz mixed glacé fruits, such as pineapple, cherries and orange
* 55 g/2 oz whole shelled nuts, such as Brazil nuts, almonds and walnuts

# Orange Cheesecake Gateau

1. Preheat the oven to 180°C/350°F/Gas Mark 4. Grease and line two 23-cm/9-inch sandwich cake tins.

2. Sift the flour and baking powder into a large bowl and add the butter, caster sugar, eggs and orange flower water. Beat well until the mixture is smooth, then stir in the orange juice.

3. Spoon the mixture into the prepared tins and smooth the surfaces with a palette knife. Bake in the preheated oven for 25–30 minutes, or until risen and golden brown.

4. Leave to cool in the tins for 5 minutes, then turn out and finish cooling on a wire rack.

5. Beat together all the filling ingredients until smooth, then spread about a third over one cake. Spoon the remainder into a piping bag fitted with a large star nozzle and pipe swirls around the edge of the cake.

6. Place the second cake on top. Pipe the remaining frosting around the top edge. Fill the centre with orange slices and brush with maple syrup.

**Serves 8–10**

- oil or melted butter, for greasing
- 175 g/6 oz plain white flour
- 1 tbsp baking powder
- 175 g/6 oz unsalted butter, softened
- 175 g/6 oz golden caster sugar
- 3 eggs, beaten
- 1 tsp orange flower water
- 2 tbsp orange juice

Filling
600 g/1 lb 5 oz mascarpone cheese
finely grated rind of 1 orange
1 tbsp orange juice
55 g/2 oz icing sugar
1 tsp orange flower water

Topping
1 orange, peeled and sliced
maple syrup, for brushing

# Walnut Torte

1. Preheat the oven to 180°C/350°F/Gas Mark 4. Grease two 20-cm/8-inch sandwich cake tins and line the bases with baking paper.

2. Sift the flour and baking powder into a large bowl and add the butter, caster sugar, eggs and vanilla extract. Beat well until the mixture is smooth, then stir in the milk and 40 g/1½ oz of the chopped walnuts.

3. Divide the mixture between the prepared tins and smooth the surfaces with a palette knife. Bake in the preheated oven for 25–30 minutes, or until risen, firm and golden brown.

4. Leave to cool in the tins for 2–3 minutes, then turn out and finish cooling on a wire rack. Slice each cake in half horizontally, to make four layers in total.

5. For the frosting, beat together the butter, icing sugar and cream until smooth. Spread about half the frosting over the top of three of the cakes and sandwich them together, placing the plain one on top.

6. Spread half the remaining frosting over the sides of the cake to cover thinly and press over the remaining chopped walnuts. Brush the apricot jam over the top of the cake. Spoon the remaining frosting into a piping bag fitted with a star nozzle and pipe swirls of frosting around the top edge of the cake. Decorate the top with walnut halves.

## Serves 8–10

* oil or melted butter, for greasing
* 175 g/6 oz plain white flour
* 1 tbsp baking powder
* 175 g/6 oz unsalted butter, softened
* 175 g/6 oz golden caster sugar
* 3 eggs, beaten
* 1 tsp vanilla extract
* 2 tbsp milk
* 125 g/4½ oz walnuts, finely chopped, plus extra walnut halves to decorate
* 3 tbsp apricot jam, warmed

### Frosting
175 g/6 oz unsalted butter
350 g/12 oz icing sugar, sifted
100 ml/3½ fl oz single cream

# 18

# Boozy Coffee Meringue

1. Preheat the oven to 160°C/325°F/Gas Mark 3. Grease and line a 25-cm/10-inch round cake tin.

2. Sift the flour and baking powder into a large bowl and add the butter, muscovado sugar, eggs and coffee extract. Beat well until the mixture is smooth, then stir in the milk.

3. Spoon the mixture into the prepared tin and smooth the surface with a palette knife. Bake in the preheated oven for 40–50 minutes, or until risen, firm and golden brown.

4. Leave to cool in the tin for 2–3 minutes, then turn out onto a flameproof serving plate. Prick the cake all over with a skewer, then sprinkle with the liqueur.

5. For the meringue topping, place the egg whites in a clean bowl and whisk with a hand-held electric mixer until thick enough to hold soft peaks. Gradually add the caster sugar, whisking vigorously after each addition, then whisk in the coffee extract.

6. Spoon the meringue on top of the cake and spread into peaks and swirls with a palette knife. Use a chef's blowtorch to brown the meringue or place the cake under a hot grill for 2–3 minutes, or until just browned but still soft inside. Cut into slices and serve.

**Serves 6–8**

* oil or melted butter, for greasing
* 175 g/6 oz plain white flour
* 1 tbsp baking powder
* 175 g/6 oz unsalted butter, softened
* 175 g/6 oz light muscovado sugar
* 3 eggs, beaten
* 1 tsp coffee extract
* 2 tbsp milk
  3 tbsp coffee liqueur

**Meringue topping**
3 egg whites
150 g/5½ oz caster sugar
1½ tsp coffee extract

# Strawberry Mousse Cake

1. Preheat the oven to 160°C/325°F/Gas Mark 3. Grease and line a 23 cm/9-inch round spring-release cake tin.

2. Sift the flour and baking powder into a large bowl and add the butter, sugar, eggs and vanilla extract. Beat well until the mixture is smooth, then stir in the milk.

3. Spoon the mixture into the prepared tin and smooth the surface with a palette knife. Bake in the preheated oven for 45–55 minutes, or until risen and golden brown.

4. Leave to cool in the tin for 5 minutes, then turn out and finish cooling on a wire rack. Cut the sponge in half horizontally and place one half back in the cake tin.

5. For the filling, dissolve the gelatine in the orange juice in a small bowl placed in a saucepan of hot water. In a blender or processor, purée 400 g/14 oz of the strawberries with the sugar. Whip the cream until thick enough to hold its shape. Quickly stir the gelatine mixture into the strawberry mixture, then fold in the cream.

6. Pour the mixture into the tin and place the second half of the cake on top. Chill in the refrigerator until set. Turn out the cake and spread the top with the warmed redcurrant jelly. Decorate with the remaining strawberries.

**Serves 8–10**

* oil or melted butter, for greasing
* 175 g/6 oz plain white flour
* 1 tbsp baking powder
* 175 g/6 oz unsalted butter, softened
* 175 g/6 oz golden caster sugar
* 3 eggs, beaten
* 1 tsp vanilla extract
* 2 tbsp milk

**Filling and topping**
4 tsp powdered gelatine
3 tbsp orange juice
550 g/1 lb 4 oz fresh strawberries
3 tbsp golden caster sugar
400 ml/14 fl oz double cream
100 g/3½ oz redcurrant jelly, warmed

# Blueberry Swirl Gateau

1. Preheat the oven to 160°C/325°F/Gas Mark 3. Grease three 19-cm/7½-inch sandwich cake tins and line the bases with baking paper.

2. Sift the flour and baking powder into a large bowl and add the butter, caster sugar, eggs and orange flower water. Beat well until the mixture is smooth, then stir in the orange juice.

3. Spoon the mixture into the prepared tins and smooth the surfaces with a palette knife. Bake in the preheated oven for 20–25 minutes, or until risen, firm and golden brown.

4. Leave to cool in the tins for 2–3 minutes, then turn out and finish cooling on a wire rack.

5. For the frosting, beat together the soft cheese and icing sugar until smooth. Transfer about two thirds of the mixture to a separate bowl and stir in 140 g/5 oz of the blueberries, then use this to sandwich the cakes together.

6. Rub the remaining blueberries through a fine sieve to make a smooth purée. Spread the remaining frosting on top of the cake and swirl the blueberry purée through it.

**Serves 8–10**

- ✳ oil or melted butter, for greasing
- ✳ 175 g/6 oz plain white flour
- ✳ 1 tbsp baking powder
- ✳ 175 g/6 oz unsalted butter, softened
- ✳ 175 g/6 oz caster sugar
- ✳ 3 eggs, beaten
- ✳ 1 tsp orange flower water
- ✳ 2 tbsp orange juice

**Filling and frosting**
200 g/7 oz full-fat soft cheese
100 g/3½ oz icing sugar, sifted
225 g/8 oz fresh blueberries

# Dainty

# 21

# Jammy Cupcakes

1. Preheat the oven to 190°C/375°F/Gas Mark 5. Place 28 paper cases into bun tins or put double-layer paper cases onto baking trays.

2. Sift the flour, baking powder and custard powder into a large bowl and add the butter, caster sugar, eggs and vanilla extract. Beat well until the mixture is smooth.

3. Divide the mixture between the paper cases and place a half teaspoonful of jam onto the centre of each, without pressing down.

4. Bake in the preheated oven for 15–20 minutes, or until risen, firm and golden brown. Transfer the cupcakes to a wire rack to cool. Dust with icing sugar when cold.

**Makes 28**

* 175 g/6 oz plain white flour
* 1 tbsp baking powder
  1 tbsp custard powder
* 175 g/6 oz unsalted butter, softened
* 175 g/6 oz golden caster sugar
* 3 eggs, beaten
* 1 tsp vanilla extract
  70 g/2½ oz raspberry jam
  icing sugar, for dusting

# 22

# Fairy Flyaway Cupcakes

1. Preheat the oven to 190°C/375°F/Gas Mark 5. Place 28 paper cases into bun tins or put double-layer paper cases onto baking trays.

2. Sift the flour and baking powder into a large bowl and add the butter, caster sugar, eggs and vanilla extract. Beat well until the mixture is smooth, then stir in enough of the milk to make a soft dropping consistency.

3. Divide the mixture between the paper cases. Bake in the preheated oven for 15–20 minutes, or until risen, firm and golden brown. Transfer the cupcakes to a wire rack to cool.

4. For the buttercream, beat together the butter, icing sugar and vanilla extract until smooth.

5. Use a serrated knife to cut a round from the top of each cupcake, then cut each round in half. Spread or pipe a little of the buttercream on top of each cake, then press the pieces of cake into it to resemble butterfly wings. Decorate with the coloured sprinkles.

**Makes 28**

- ✳ 175 g/6 oz plain white flour
- ✳ 1 tbsp baking powder
- ✳ 175 g/6 oz unsalted butter, softened
- ✳ 175 g/6 oz golden caster sugar
- ✳ 3 eggs, beaten
- ✳ 1 tsp vanilla extract
  about 1 tbsp milk
  coloured sprinkles, to decorate

**Buttercream**
100 g/3½ oz unsalted butter, softened
200 g/7 oz icing sugar
½ tsp vanilla extract

# Chocolate Flake Cupcakes

1 Preheat the oven to 190°C/375°F/Gas Mark 5. Place 30 paper cases into bun tins or put double-layer paper cases onto baking trays.

2 Sift the flour and baking powder into a large bowl and add the butter, sugar, eggs and vanilla extract. Beat well until the mixture is smooth. Mix the milk with the cocoa powder and stir into the mixture.

3 Divide the mixture between the paper cases and sprinkle with about a quarter of the crumbled chocolate. Bake in the preheated oven for 15–20 minutes, or until risen, firm and golden brown. Transfer the cupcakes to a wire rack to cool.

4 When the cupcakes are cold, brush the tops with apricot jam and sprinkle with the remaining crumbled chocolate.

**Makes 30**

* 175 g/6 oz plain white flour
* 1 tbsp baking powder
* 175 g/6 oz unsalted butter, softened
* 175 g/6 oz golden caster sugar
* 3 eggs, beaten
* 1 tsp vanilla extract
* 2 tbsp milk
  1 tbsp cocoa powder
  70 g/2½ oz chocolate flake bars, crumbled
  3 tbsp apricot jam, warmed

# Gingerbread Cupcakes

1. Preheat the oven to 190°C/375°F/Gas Mark 5. Place 30 paper cases into bun tins or put double-layer paper cases onto baking trays.

2. Sift the flour, baking powder, ginger and cinnamon into a large bowl and add the butter, muscovado sugar, eggs and vanilla extract. Beat well until the mixture is smooth.

3. Divide the mixture between the paper cases. Bake in the preheated oven for 15–20 minutes, or until risen, firm and golden brown. Transfer the cupcakes to a wire rack to cool.

4. For the frosting, beat together the butter, icing sugar and orange juice until smooth. Spoon a little frosting on top of each cupcake and top with the crystallised ginger.

**Makes 30**

* 175 g/6 oz plain white flour
* 1 tbsp baking powder
  2 tsp ground ginger
  1 tsp ground cinnamon
* 175 g/6 oz unsalted butter, softened
* 175 g/6 oz dark muscovado sugar
* 3 eggs, beaten
* 1 tsp vanilla extract
  chopped crystallised ginger, to decorate

Frosting
85 g/3 oz unsalted butter, softened
150 g/5½ oz icing sugar, sifted
3 tbsp orange juice

# 25

# Maple Pecan Cupcakes

1. Preheat the oven to 190°C/375°F/Gas Mark 5. Place 30 paper cases into bun tins or put double-layer paper cases onto baking trays.

2. Sift the flour and baking powder into a large bowl and add the butter, sugar, maple syrup, eggs and vanilla extract. Beat well until the mixture is smooth, then stir in the pecan nuts.

3. Divide the mixture between the paper cases. For the topping, mix together the pecans, flour, sugar and melted butter to make a crumbly mixture and spoon a little on top of each cupcake.

4. Bake in the preheated oven for 15–20 minutes, or until risen, firm and golden brown. Transfer the cupcakes to a wire rack to cool.

**Makes 30**

* 175 g/6 oz plain white flour
* 1 tbsp baking powder
* 175 g/6 oz unsalted butter, softened
  115 g/4 oz light muscovado sugar
  4 tbsp maple syrup
* 3 eggs, beaten
* 1 tsp vanilla extract
  30 g/1 oz pecan nuts, finely chopped

Topping
40 g/1½ oz pecan nuts, finely chopped
2 tbsp plain white flour
2 tbsp light muscovado sugar
2 tbsp melted butter

# Cherry Cupcakes with Ricotta Frosting

1. Preheat the oven to 190°C/375°F/Gas Mark 5. Place 28 paper cases into bun tins or put double-layer paper cases onto baking trays.

2. Stir a tablespoon of the flour into the chopped glacé cherries. Sift the remaining flour with the baking powder and cornflour into a large bowl and add the butter, caster sugar, eggs and vanilla extract. Beat well until the mixture is smooth, then stir in the glacé cherry and flour mixture.

3. Divide the mixture between the paper cases. Bake in the preheated oven for 15–20 minutes, or until risen, firm and golden brown. Transfer the cupcakes to a wire rack to cool.

4. For the frosting, mix the ricotta with the icing sugar and vanilla extract, then spoon a little on top of each cupcake. Top each with half a glacé cherry.

**Makes 28**

* 175 g/6 oz plain white flour
  70 g/2½ oz glacé cherries, chopped
* 1 tbsp baking powder
  1 tbsp cornflour
* 175 g/6 oz unsalted butter, softened
* 175 g/6 oz caster sugar
* 3 eggs, beaten
* 1 tsp vanilla extract
  14 glacé cherries, halved, to decorate

Frosting
250 g/9 oz ricotta cheese
70 g/2½ oz icing sugar
½ tsp vanilla extract

# Raspberry Ripple Cupcakes

1. Preheat the oven to 190°C/375°F/Gas Mark 5. Place 32 paper cases into bun tins or put double-layer paper cases onto baking trays.

2. Sift the flour, baking powder and cornflour into a large bowl and add the butter, caster sugar, eggs and almond extract. Beat well until the mixture is smooth. Mash the raspberries lightly with a fork, then fold into the mixture.

3. Divide the mixture between the paper cases. Bake in the preheated oven for 15–20 minutes, or until risen, firm and golden brown.

4. Transfer the cupcakes to a wire rack to cool. Sprinkle with vanilla sugar before serving.

**Makes 32**

* 175 g/6 oz plain white flour
* 1 tbsp baking powder
  1 tbsp cornflour
* 175 g/6 oz unsalted butter, softened
* 175 g/6 oz caster sugar
* 3 eggs, beaten
* 1 tsp almond extract
  200 g/7 oz fresh raspberries
  vanilla sugar, for sprinkling

# 28

# Blueberry Cupcakes with Soured Cream Frosting

1. Preheat the oven to 190°C/375°F/Gas Mark 5. Place 30 paper cases into bun tins or put double-layer paper cases onto baking trays.

2. Sift the flour and baking powder into a large bowl and add the butter, caster sugar, eggs and vanilla extract. Beat well until the mixture is smooth, then stir in the orange rind and 100g/3½ oz of the blueberries.

3. Divide the mixture between the paper cases. Bake in the preheated oven for 15–20 minutes, or until risen, firm and golden brown. Transfer the cupcakes to a wire rack to cool.

4. For the frosting, stir the soured cream into the icing sugar and mix well until smooth. Spoon a little frosting on top of each cupcake and top with the remaining blueberries. Leave to set.

**Makes 30**

* 175 g/6 oz plain white flour
* 1 tbsp baking powder
* 175 g/6 oz unsalted butter, softened
* 175 g/6 oz caster sugar
* 3 eggs, beaten
* 1 tsp vanilla extract
  finely grated rind of ½ orange
  150 g/5½ oz fresh blueberries

**Frosting**
3 tbsp soured cream
150 g/5½ oz icing sugar, sifted

# Vanilla Hazelnut Yogurt Cupcakes

1. Preheat the oven to 190°C/375°F/Gas Mark 5. Place 26 paper cases into bun tins or put double-layer paper cases onto baking trays.

2. Sift the flour, cornflour and baking powder into a large bowl and add the yogurt, caster sugar, eggs and vanilla extract. Beat well until the mixture is smooth, then stir in the finely chopped hazelnuts.

3. Divide the mixture between the paper cases. Bake in the preheated oven for 15–20 minutes, or until risen, firm and golden brown. Transfer the cupcakes to a wire rack to cool.

4. For the topping, mix the icing sugar and yogurt until smooth, then drizzle over the cupcakes and scatter over the roughly chopped hazelnuts. Leave to set.

**Makes 26**

* 175 g/6 oz plain white flour
2 tsp cornflour
* 1 tbsp baking powder
* 175 g/6 oz natural yogurt
* 175 g/6 oz golden caster sugar
* 3 eggs, beaten
* 1 tsp vanilla extract
40 g/1½ oz hazelnuts, finely chopped

Topping
100 g/3½ oz icing sugar, sifted
40 g/1½ oz natural yogurt
25 g/1 oz hazelnuts, roughly chopped

# 30

# Coffee Fudge Cupcakes

1. Preheat the oven to 190°C/375°F/Gas Mark 5. Place 28 paper cases into bun tins or put double-layer paper cases onto baking trays.

2. Sift the flour and baking powder into a large bowl and add the butter, caster sugar, eggs and coffee extract. Beat well until the mixture is smooth, then beat in the milk.

3. Divide the mixture between the paper cases. Bake in the preheated oven for 15–20 minutes, or until risen, firm and golden brown. Transfer the cupcakes to a wire rack to cool.

4. For the frosting, place the butter, muscovado sugar, cream and coffee extract in a saucepan over a medium heat and stir until melted and smooth. Bring to the boil and boil, stirring, for 2 minutes. Remove from the heat and beat in the icing sugar.

5. Stir the frosting until smooth and thick, then spoon into a piping bag fitted with a large star nozzle. Pipe a swirl of frosting on top of each cupcake and top with a coffee bean.

**Makes 28**

* 175 g/6 oz plain white flour
* 1 tbsp baking powder
* 175 g/6 oz unsalted butter, softened
* 175 g/6 oz caster sugar
* 3 eggs, beaten
* 1 tsp coffee extract
* 2 tbsp milk
  chocolate-covered coffee beans, to decorate

**Frosting**
55 g/2 oz unsalted butter
115 g/4 oz light muscovado sugar
2 tbsp single cream or milk
½ tsp coffee extract
400 g/14 oz icing sugar, sifted

# Fruity

# 31

# Rhubarb & Ginger Cake

1. Preheat the oven to 180°C/350°F/Gas Mark 4. Grease and line a 23-cm/9-inch square deep cake tin.

2. Sift the flour and baking powder into a large bowl and add the butter, caster sugar, eggs and vanilla extract. Beat well until the mixture is smooth.

3. Spoon the mixture into the prepared tin and smooth the surface with a palette knife. Stir the cornflour into the rhubarb, then add the ginger and scatter evenly over the cake mixture.

4. Bake in the preheated oven for 50–60 minutes, or until risen, firm and golden brown. Leave to cool in the tin for about 10 minutes, then turn out and finish cooling on a wire rack.

5. For the icing, mix the icing sugar with the ginger syrup until smooth, then drizzle over the cake. Leave until set before cutting into slices.

**Serves 8**

* oil or melted butter, for greasing
* 175 g/6 oz plain white flour
  2 tsp baking powder
* 175 g/6 oz unsalted butter, softened
* 175 g/6 oz caster sugar
* 3 eggs, beaten
* 1 tsp vanilla extract
  1 tbsp cornflour
  200 g/7 oz pink rhubarb, cut into 1-cm/½-inch slices
  30 g/1 oz stem ginger, finely chopped

Icing
3 tbsp icing sugar
3 tsp stem ginger syrup (from the jar)

# 32

# Pear & Hazelnut Streusel Cake

1. Preheat the oven to 180°C/350°F/Gas Mark 4. Grease and line a 23-cm/9-inch round spring-release cake tin.

2. For the streusel topping, mix the chopped hazelnuts, muscovado sugar, flour, cinnamon and melted butter in a small bowl with a fork to make a crumbly mixture.

3. Sift the flour and baking powder into a large bowl and add the butter, caster sugar, eggs and vanilla extract. Beat well until the mixture is smooth, then stir in the ground hazelnuts and half the chopped pears.

4. Spoon the mixture into the prepared tin and smooth the surface with a palette knife. Scatter over the remaining chopped pears and spread level. Sprinkle the streusel topping evenly over the cake.

5. Bake in the preheated oven for about 1 hour, or until risen and firm. Leave to cool in the tin for 2–3 minutes, then remove the sides of the tin and finish cooling on a wire rack.

**Serves 8**

※ oil or melted butter, for greasing

※ 175 g/6 oz plain white flour

2 tsp baking powder

※ 175 g/6 oz unsalted butter, softened

※ 175 g/6 oz golden caster sugar

※ 3 eggs, beaten

※ 1 tsp vanilla extract

55 g/2 oz ground hazelnuts

2 firm ripe pears, peeled, cored and finely chopped

**Streusel topping**

50 g/1¾ oz toasted hazelnuts, finely chopped

40 g/1½ oz dark muscovado sugar

3 tbsp plain white flour

½ tsp ground cinnamon

25 g/1 oz unsalted butter, melted

# Chewy Date & Sesame Slices

1. Preheat the oven to 180°C/350°F/Gas Mark 4. Grease and line a 30 x 23-cm/12 x 9-inch rectangular traybake tin.

2. Place the dates and orange juice in a saucepan and heat, stirring occasionally, until boiling. Reduce the heat and simmer gently for about 5 minutes, until the liquid is absorbed. Remove from the heat and leave to cool.

3. Sift the flours and baking powder into a large bowl, adding any bran left in the sieve. Add the butter, sugar, eggs and vanilla extract. Beat well until the mixture is smooth, then stir in the soaked dates.

4. Spoon the mixture into the prepared tin and smooth the surface with a palette knife. Sprinkle the sesame seeds evenly over the top. Bake in the preheated oven for 25–30 minutes, or until risen, firm and golden brown.

5. Leave to cool in the tin, then cut into slices when firm.

**Makes 12**

* oil or melted butter, for greasing
* 200 g/7 oz pitted dates, roughly chopped
* 4 tbsp orange juice
* 85 g/3 oz plain white flour
* 85 g/3 oz plain wholemeal flour
* 1½ tsp baking powder
* 175 g/6 oz unsalted butter, softened
* 175 g/6 oz dark muscovado sugar
* 3 eggs, beaten
* 1 tsp vanilla extract
* 3 tbsp sesame seeds

# Honeyed Apple Slices

1. Preheat the oven to 180°C/350°F/Gas Mark 4. Grease and line a 30 x 23-cm/12 x 9-inch rectangular traybake tin.

2. Sift the flour, baking powder and allspice into a large bowl and add the butter, sugar, eggs and vanilla extract. Beat well until the mixture is smooth, then stir in the apple juice.

3. Spoon the mixture into the prepared tin and smooth the surface with a palette knife. Core and slice the apples and arrange them, overlapping, on top of the cake mixture, without pressing into the mix. Brush lightly with half the honey.

4. Bake in the preheated oven for 30–35 minutes, or until risen, firm and golden brown. Leave to cool in the tin for about 15 minutes, until firm, then cut into slices and finish cooling on a wire rack.

5. Brush with the remaining honey before serving.

**Makes 12**

* oil or melted butter, for greasing
* 175 g/6 oz plain white flour
  2 tsp baking powder
  ½ tsp ground allspice
* 175 g/6 oz unsalted butter, softened
* 175 g/6 oz caster sugar
* 3 eggs, beaten
* 1 tsp vanilla extract
* 2 tbsp apple juice
  4 red-skinned apples
  3 tbsp clear honey, warmed

# 35

# Tropical Fruit Ring

1. Preheat the oven to 160°C/325°F/Gas Mark 3. Grease a 1.5-litre/2¾-pint ring cake tin, preferably non-stick. Stir the lime juice into the dried tropical fruit and leave to soak for 15 minutes.

2. Sift the flour and baking powder into a large bowl and add the butter, caster sugar, eggs and vanilla extract. Beat well until the mixture is smooth, then stir in the soaked fruit.

3. Spoon the mixture into the prepared tin and level the surface with a palette knife. Bake in the preheated oven for 40–50 minutes, or until risen, firm and golden brown. Leave to cool in the tin for 10 minutes, then turn out and finish cooling on a wire rack.

4. For the icing, sift the icing sugar into a bowl, add the lime juice and stir until smooth. Spoon the icing over the cake and decorate with dried tropical fruit. Leave to set before slicing.

**Serves 12**

* oil or melted butter, for greasing
* 2 tbsp lime juice
  100 g/3½ oz dried tropical fruit, such as mango, papaya and/or pineapple, finely chopped, plus extra to decorate
* 175 g/6 oz plain white flour
  2½ tsp baking powder
* 175 g/6 oz unsalted butter, softened
* 175 g/6 oz golden caster sugar
* 3 eggs, beaten
* 1 tsp vanilla extract

**Icing**
70 g/2½ oz icing sugar
1 tbsp lime juice

# 36

# Banana & Carrot Squares

1. Preheat the oven to 160°C/325°F/Gas Mark 3. Grease and line a 23-cm/9-inch square cake tin.

2. Sift the flour, baking powder and nutmeg into a bowl and add the butter, caster sugar and eggs. Beat well until smooth, then stir in the lemon juice, banana, carrots and walnuts.

3. Spoon the mixture into the prepared tin and smooth the surface with a palette knife. Bake in the preheated oven for 45–55 minutes, or until well risen, firm and golden brown.

4. Leave to cool in the tin for 5 minutes, then turn out onto a wire rack to finish cooling. Cut into squares when cold.

5. For the frosting, mix the ricotta with the icing sugar and lemon rind in a small bowl. Pipe or spoon a little frosting on top of each square of cake, top with a banana chip and sprinkle with nutmeg.

**Makes 16**

* oil or melted butter, for greasing
* 175 g/6 oz plain white flour
* 1 tbsp baking powder
* 1 tsp ground nutmeg
* 175 g/6 oz unsalted butter, softened
* 175 g/6 oz golden caster sugar
* 3 eggs, beaten
* 1 tbsp lemon juice
* 1 banana, mashed
* 140 g/5 oz carrots, coarsely grated
* 40 g/1½ oz walnuts, finely chopped
* dried banana chips and freshly grated nutmeg, to decorate

Frosting
250 g/9 oz ricotta cheese
70 g/2½ oz icing sugar
finely grated rind of ½ lemon

# Chunky Orange & Peanut Squares

1. Preheat the oven to 160°C/325°F/Gas Mark 3. Grease and line a 23-cm/9-inch square cake tin.

2. Finely grate the rind from the orange and reserve. Use a sharp knife to cut off all the peel and white pith, then cut the flesh into small chunks.

3. Sift the flour and baking powder into a large bowl and add the butter, peanut butter, caster sugar, eggs and vanilla extract. Beat well until the mixture is smooth, then stir in the orange rind and orange chunks.

4. Spoon the mixture into the prepared tin and smooth the surface with a palette knife. Bake in the preheated oven for 40–50 minutes, or until risen, firm and golden brown. Leave to cool in the tin for about 10 minutes, then turn out and finish cooling on a wire rack.

5. For the icing, mix together the peanut butter, orange juice and icing sugar, then spread over the cooled cake. Cut into squares before serving.

**Makes 9**

* oil or melted butter, for greasing
* 1 orange
* 175 g/6 oz plain white flour
* 1½ tsp baking powder
* 100 g/3½ oz unsalted butter, softened
* 70 g/3 oz crunchy peanut butter
* 175 g/6 oz caster sugar
* 3 eggs, beaten
* 1 tsp vanilla extract

**Icing**
* 55 g/2 oz crunchy peanut butter
* 2 tbsp orange juice
* 55 g/2 oz icing sugar

# 38

# Kiwi Fruit Cake with Lemon Frosting

1. Preheat the oven to 160°C/325°F/Gas Mark 3. Grease and line a 1.2-litre/2-pint loaf tin.

2. Sift the flour and baking powder into a large bowl and add the butter, caster sugar, eggs and vanilla extract. Beat well until the mixture is smooth, then stir in half the chopped kiwi fruit.

3. Spoon the mixture into the prepared tin and smooth the surface with a palette knife. Scatter over the remaining chopped kiwi fruit. Bake in the preheated oven for about 1 hour, or until risen, firm and golden brown.

4. Leave to cool in the tin for 10 minutes, then turn out and finish cooling on a wire rack.

5. For the frosting, beat together the cream cheese, lemon rind and icing sugar until smooth. Spread the frosting over the cake and top with kiwi fruit slices.

**Serves 8**

* oil or melted butter, for greasing
* 175 g/6 oz plain white flour
  2 tsp baking powder
* 175 g/6 oz unsalted butter, softened
* 175 g/6 oz caster sugar
* 3 eggs, beaten
* 1 tsp vanilla extract
  2 kiwi fruit, peeled and chopped into 1-cm/½-inch dice, plus extra slices to decorate

Frosting
55 g/2 oz cream cheese
1 tbsp grated lemon rind
115 g/4 oz icing sugar

# Chunky Apricot Loaf

1. Preheat the oven to 160°C/325°F/Gas Mark 3. Grease and line a 1.2-litre/2-pint loaf tin.

2. Sift the flour and baking powder into a large bowl and add the butter, sugar, eggs and almond extract. Beat well until the mixture is smooth, then stir in the orange juice and 150 g/5½ oz of the dried apricots.

3. Spoon the mixture into the prepared tin and smooth the surface with a palette knife. Sprinkle with the remaining dried apricots. Bake in the preheated oven for about 1 hour, or until risen, firm and golden brown.

4. Leave to cool in the tin for 10 minutes, then turn out and finish cooling on a wire rack.

5. Warm the apricot jam with the lemon juice and brush lightly over the cake top to serve.

**Serves 8**

* oil or melted butter, for greasing
  250 g/9 oz plain white flour
  2 tsp baking powder
* 175 g/6 oz unsalted butter, softened
* 175 g/6 oz golden caster sugar
* 3 eggs, beaten
* 1 tsp almond extract
* 2 tbsp orange juice
  200 g/7 oz ready-to-eat dried apricots, chopped
  3 tbsp apricot jam
  1 tbsp lemon juice

# Chocolate & Cherry Gateau

1. Preheat the oven to 180°C/350°F/Gas Mark 4. Grease two 20-cm/8-inch sandwich cake tins and line the bases with baking paper.

2. Sift the flour, cocoa and baking powder into a large bowl and add the butter, caster sugar, eggs and vanilla extract. Beat well until the mixture is smooth, then stir in the milk.

3. Divide the mixture between the prepared tins and smooth the tops with a palette knife. Bake in the oven for 25–30 minutes, or until risen and firm to the touch. Leave to cool in the tins for 2–3 minutes, then turn out and finish cooling on wire racks.

4. When the cakes are cold, sprinkle with the kirsch, if using. Whip the cream with the icing sugar until thick, then spread about a third over the top of one of the cakes. Spread the cherries over the cream and place the second cake on top.

5. Spread the remaining cream over the top and sides of the cake and decorate with grated chocolate and fresh whole cherries.

**Serves 8**

* oil or melted butter, for greasing
* 150 g/5½ oz plain white flour
* 2 tbsp cocoa powder
* 1 tbsp baking powder
* 175 g/6 oz unsalted butter, softened
* 175 g/6 oz golden caster sugar
* 3 eggs, beaten
* 1 tsp vanilla extract
* 2 tbsp milk
* 3 tbsp kirsch or brandy (optional)
* grated chocolate and fresh whole cherries, to decorate

**Filling and topping**
* 450 ml/16 fl oz double or whipping cream
* 2 tbsp icing sugar
* 225 g/8 oz fresh or frozen dark red cherries, pitted

# Warming

# 41

# Plum Sponge Bake

1. Preheat the oven to 160°C/325°F/Gas Mark 3. Grease and line a 32 x 23-cm/13 x 9-inch rectangular cake tin.

2. Sift the flour and baking powder into a large bowl and add the butter, sugar, eggs and almond extract. Beat well until the mixture is smooth, then stir in the ground almonds.

3. Spoon the mixture into the prepared tin and smooth the surface with a palette knife. Arrange the plum quarters, skin-side down, over the mixture, without pressing them in, then scatter over the flaked almonds and demerara sugar.

4. Bake in the preheated oven for 50–60 minutes, or until risen and golden brown. Cut into squares and serve warm with cream or yogurt.

**Serves 6**

* oil or melted butter, for greasing
* 175 g/6 oz plain white flour
  2 tsp baking powder
* 175 g/6 oz unsalted butter, softened
* 175 g/6 oz golden caster sugar
* 3 eggs, beaten
* 1 tsp almond extract
  70 g/2½ oz ground almonds
  8–10 large red plums, quartered and stoned
  3 tbsp flaked almonds
  2 tbsp demerara sugar
  cream or yogurt, to serve

# Toffee Apple Upside-down Cake

1. Preheat the oven to 180°C/350°F/Gas Mark 4. Grease a 23-cm/9-inch round deep cake tin with a solid base.

2. For the toffee apple topping, place the butter and sugar in a heavy-based saucepan with the water and heat gently until melted, then bring to the boil. Reduce the heat and cook, stirring, until it turns to a deep golden caramel colour. Pour quickly into the cake tin, tilting to cover the base evenly.

3. Peel, core and thickly slice the apples, toss with the lemon juice and spread evenly over the base of the cake tin.

4. Sift the flour and baking powder into a large bowl and add the butter, sugar, eggs and vanilla extract. Beat well until the mixture is smooth, then stir in the lemon rind.

5. Spoon the mixture over the apples and smooth the surface with a palette knife. Bake in the preheated oven for 40–50 minutes, or until risen and golden brown.

6. Leave to cool in the tin for 2–3 minutes, then turn out carefully onto a warmed serving plate. Serve with cream.

**Serves 6**

* oil or melted butter, for greasing
* 175 g/6 oz plain white flour
* 1 tbsp baking powder
* 175 g/6 oz unsalted butter, softened
* 175 g/6 oz golden caster sugar
* 3 eggs, beaten
* 1 tsp vanilla extract
  finely grated rind of 1 lemon
  cream, to serve

**Toffee apple topping**
55 g/2 oz unsalted butter
100 g/3½ oz caster sugar
1 tbsp water
4 eating apples
2 tbsp lemon juice

# Mocha Puddings M

1. Preheat the oven to 200°C/400°F/Gas Mark 6. Grease and line six 200-ml/7-fl oz individual metal pudding basins.

2. Sift the flour, cocoa and baking powder into a large bowl and add the butter, sugar, eggs and coffee extract. Beat well until the mixture is smooth.

3. Spoon the mixture into the prepared pudding basins. Place a square of chocolate on top of each. Bake in the preheated oven for 20–25 minutes, or until risen and firm to the touch.

4. For the sauce, place the cream, chocolate and coffee extract in a small saucepan and heat gently without boiling, stirring, until melted and smooth. Turn out the puddings and serve with the sauce poured over them.

**Makes 6**

* oil or melted butter, for greasing
* 175 g/6 oz plain white flour
  2 tbsp cocoa powder
  2 tsp baking powder
* 175 g/6 oz unsalted butter, softened
* 175 g/6 oz light muscovado sugar
* 3 eggs, beaten
* 1 tsp coffee extract
  6 small squares plain chocolate

**Sauce**
250 ml/9 fl oz single cream
100 g/3½ oz plain chocolate, broken into pieces
1 tsp coffee extract

# Lemon Surprise Cakes

1. Preheat the oven to 180°C/350°F/Gas Mark 4. Grease six 200-ml/7-fl oz ovenproof teacups or ramekins and place in a roasting tin.

2. Sift the flour and baking powder into a large bowl and add the butter, sugar and egg yolks. Beat well until the mixture is smooth, then stir in the lemon rind, lemon juice and milk. In a separate bowl, whisk the egg whites until they hold stiff peaks. Fold into the creamed mixture.

3. Spoon the mixture into the prepared teacups or ramekins. Pour enough hot water into the tin to come halfway up the sides of the teacups or ramekins. Bake in the preheated oven for 30–35 minutes, or until risen, firm and golden brown.

4. Transfer the teacups or ramekins to warmed serving plates. There should be a light custard layer under the sponge.

**Makes 6**

* oil or melted butter, for greasing
* 175 g/6 oz plain white flour
* 1 tbsp baking powder
* 175 g/6 oz unsalted butter, softened
* 175 g/6 oz caster sugar
* 3 eggs, separated
  finely grated rind and juice of 2 lemons
  150 ml/5 fl oz milk

# 45

# Peach & Cinnamon Cobbler

1. Preheat the oven to 160°C/325°F/Gas Mark 3. Grease a 23-cm/9-inch round spring-release cake tin and line the base with baking paper.

2. Sift the flour, baking powder and cinnamon into a large bowl and add the butter, sugar, eggs and vanilla extract. Beat well until the mixture is smooth.

3. Spoon half the mixture into the prepared tin and smooth the surface with a palette knife. Arrange the peaches on top. Stir the cornflakes lightly into the remaining mixture, then drop spoonfuls of the mix over the peaches.

4. Bake in the preheated oven for about 1 hour, or until risen, firm and golden brown. Serve hot with whipped cream.

**Serves 6**

✻ oil or melted butter,
    for greasing

✻ 175 g/6 oz plain white flour

  2 tsp baking powder

  1 tsp ground cinnamon

✻ 175 g/6 oz unsalted butter,
    softened

✻ 175 g/6 oz golden caster sugar

✻ 3 eggs, beaten

✻ 1 tsp vanilla extract

  3 ripe peaches or nectarines,
    stoned and roughly chopped

  70 g/2½ oz cornflakes,
    lightly crushed

  lightly whipped cream, to serve

# Whole Orange & Almond Cake

1. Preheat the oven to 160°C/325°F/Gas Mark 3. Grease and line a 23-cm/9-inch round deep cake tin.

2. Wash the oranges and place in a saucepan, then cover with boiling water and simmer for 1 hour, covered, until soft. Drain and leave to cool slightly, then cut the oranges in half and remove and discard any pips. Purée in a food processor or blender until smooth, then stir in the ground almonds.

3. Sift the flour and baking powder into a large bowl and add the butter, sugar, eggs and orange flower water. Beat well until the mixture is smooth. Add the orange and almond mixture and the orange juice, mixing evenly.

4. Spoon the mixture into the prepared tin and smooth the surface with a palette knife. Bake in the preheated oven for 40–50 minutes, or until firm and golden brown.

5. Leave to cool in the tin for 2–3 minutes, then turn out and serve warm, topped with flaked almonds and strips of orange zest.

**Serves 8–10**

* oil or melted butter, for greasing
  2 oranges
  55 g/2 oz ground almonds
  115 g/4 oz plain white flour
* 1 tbsp baking powder
  85 g/3 oz unsalted butter, softened
* 175 g/6 oz golden caster sugar
* 3 eggs, beaten
* 1 tsp orange flower water
* 2 tbsp orange juice
  2 tbsp toasted flaked almonds
  strips of orange zest, to decorate

# Gooey Orange Chocolate Chip Cake

1. Preheat the oven to 180°C/350°F/Gas Mark 4. Grease and line a 23-cm/9-inch square cake tin.

2. Finely grate the rind from one of the oranges and reserve. Use a sharp knife to cut off all the peel and white pith from both oranges and carefully remove the segments, reserving any spare juices to add to the sauce. Chop half the segments into small pieces.

3. Sift the flour and baking powder into a large bowl and add the butter, sugar, eggs and vanilla extract. Beat well until the mixture is smooth, then stir in the orange rind and chopped orange.

4. Spoon the mixture into the prepared tin and smooth the surface with a palette knife. Sprinkle the chocolate chips over the top, spreading to the edges. Bake in the preheated oven for 35–40 minutes or until risen, firm and golden brown.

5. For the sauce, place the chocolate, butter and orange juice in a saucepan and heat gently, stirring, until melted and smooth. Serve the cake warm, topped with the reserved orange segments and with the sauce spooned over the top.

**Serves 6**

* oil or melted butter, for greasing
* 2 oranges
* 175 g/6 oz plain white flour
* 2 tsp baking powder
* 175 g/6 oz unsalted butter, softened
* 175 g/6 oz golden caster sugar
* 3 eggs, beaten
* 1 tsp vanilla extract
* 100 g/3½ oz plain chocolate chips

**Sauce**

85 g/3 oz plain chocolate, broken into pieces

40 g/1½ oz unsalted butter

3 tbsp orange juice

# 48

# Rich Walnut Squares

1. Preheat the oven to 160°C/325°F/Gas Mark 3. Grease and line a 23-cm/9-inch square cake tin.

2. Sift the flour and baking powder into a large bowl and add the butter, sugar, eggs and coffee extract. Beat well until the mixture is smooth, then stir in the crème fraîche and chopped walnuts.

3. Spoon the mixture into the prepared tin and smooth the surface with a palette knife. Bake in the preheated oven for 40–50 minutes, or until risen and firm to the touch.

4. Leave to cool in the tin for 2–3 minutes, then turn out and cut into squares. Place the crème fraîche and maple syrup in a small saucepan and heat gently, stirring until melted and smooth.

5. Top each square of cake with a walnut half, spoon over the warm sauce and serve immediately.

**Makes 9**

* oil or melted butter, for greasing
* 175 g/6 oz plain white flour
* 1 tbsp baking powder
* 175 g/6 oz unsalted butter, softened
* 175 g/6 oz light muscovado sugar
* 3 eggs, beaten
* 1 tsp coffee extract
  2 tbsp crème fraîche
  55 g/2 oz walnuts, finely chopped, plus extra walnut halves to decorate

**Sauce**
4 tbsp crème fraîche
3 tbsp maple syrup

# Currant Slices with Spiced Apple Syrup

1. Place the currants, cinnamon stick and apple juice in a saucepan and bring to the boil. Remove from the heat and leave to stand for several hours or overnight. Drain the currants thoroughly, pressing the juices through a sieve, reserving the juices and cinnamon stick. Set aside the currants.

2. Preheat the oven to 180°C/350°F/Gas Mark 4. Grease and line a 30 x 23-cm/12 x 9-inch rectangular traybake tin.

3. Sift the flour and baking powder into a large bowl and add the butter, sugar, eggs and vanilla extract. Beat well until the mixture is smooth.

4. Stir half the reserved currants into the mixture and spoon into the prepared tin. Spread the remaining currants over the top. Bake in the preheated oven for 30–35 minutes, or until risen, firm and golden brown.

5. Meanwhile, boil the reserved juices and cinnamon stick rapidly to reduce by about half, until slightly syrupy. Discard the cinnamon stick.

6. Cut the cake into slices and serve warm with the hot syrup spooned over.

**Makes 8**

175 g/6 oz currants
1 cinnamon stick
300 ml/10 fl oz apple juice
* oil or melted butter, for greasing
* 175 g/6 oz plain white flour
2 tsp baking powder
* 175 g/6 oz unsalted butter, softened
* 175 g/6 oz caster sugar
* 3 eggs, beaten
* 1 tsp vanilla extract

# Greek Yogurt & Honey Cake

1. Preheat the oven to 160°C/325°F/Gas Mark 3. Grease a 23-cm/9-inch round cake tin and line the base with baking paper.

2. Sift the flour and baking powder into a large bowl and add the yogurt, honey, sugar, eggs and vanilla extract. Beat well until the mixture is smooth.

3. Pour the mixture into the prepared tin. Bake in the preheated oven for 45–55 minutes, or until risen, firm and golden brown.

4. Leave to cool in the tin for 2–3 minutes, then turn out onto a serving plate. For the lemon sauce, place the honey, lemon juice and butter in a small saucepan and bring to the boil. Boil for a few minutes, stirring, until reduced and syrupy.

5. Serve the cake in slices with the lemon sauce poured over.

**Serves 6–8**

- oil or melted butter, for greasing
- 175 g/6 oz plain white flour
- 1 tbsp baking powder
- 175 g/6 oz Greek-style yogurt
  100 g/3½ oz Greek honey
  75 g/2½ oz light muscovado sugar
- 3 eggs, beaten
- 1 tsp vanilla extract

**Lemon sauce**
2 tbsp Greek honey
2 tbsp lemon juice
25 g/1 oz unsalted butter